Original title:
Stem by Stem

Copyright © 2025 Creative Arts Management OÜ
All rights reserved.

Author: Miriam Kensington
ISBN HARDBACK: 978-1-80566-633-2
ISBN PAPERBACK: 978-1-80566-918-0

Echoed Growth

In a garden wide, plants play tag,
Each leaf a giggle, each root a brag.
Dandelions dance with the breeze so spry,
While tulips gossip, oh my, oh my!

A cactus wearing a sun hat bright,
Tells tales of the desert with all its might.
The daisies laugh at a bee in flight,
As they wiggle and nod in pure delight.

A sunflower winks at the cloud above,
Saying, 'Your rain can't dampen our love!'
Each sprout in the row, in a silly race,
Compete for the sun with a comical face.

So when you see a garden grown,
Remember the laughs that are often sown.
With giggles and grins shared along the way,
Nature frolics in her own funny play.

The Language of Flora

In a garden where daisies giggle,
Petunias whisper secrets with a wiggle.
Sunflowers nod at the passing bees,
While roses gossip in the gentle breeze.

The violets dance in purple hats,
While dandelions play hide-and-seek with rats.
Pansies chuckle with each sunrise,
As tulips flirt under patchy skies.

Shadows Beneath the Canopy

Under trees where squirrels play chess,
Laughter rustles in nature's dress.
Leaves tickle the grass beneath,
As sunbeams wink with a playful sheath.

Mushrooms sport polka dot hats,
And crickets tap dance, oh what chitchats!
The owls share jokes, wise and slow,
While shadows tickle the ground below.

Echoes of the Wilderness

In the woods where the echoes sing,
Bears make notes, as if they're king.
Trees chuckle at the deer's sly prance,
While frogs join in a raucous dance.

Rabbits hop like they're on a spree,
Playing tag with the bumblebee.
Nature's symphony, quite absurd,
With every chirp and chattering word.

Tapestry of Growth

In the patch where veggies all collide,
Carrots gossip while radishes hide.
Tomatoes blush with the ripening sun,
While cucumbers giggle, having fun.

Zucchini wears stripes, a fashion so bold,
Peppers yell "spicy," stories retold.
Herbs whisper secrets of flavors divine,
Crafting culinary tales, all intertwined.

Petals of Promise

In a garden full of schemes,
Petals whisper secret dreams.
Wiggly worms in funny hats,
Join the party, where they're at.

Bumblebees buzz dance around,
With wobbly moves and silly sound.
Tulips giggle as they sway,
In their own comical ballet.

A Maze of Greenery

In a maze of leafy glee,
Rabbits hop, a sight to see.
Chasing tails and sniffing air,
Lost in laughter, unaware.

A squirrel juggles acorns well,
While mushrooms giggle, can't you tell?
Nature's maze is quite the jest,
Where every turn brings more fun zest.

The Dance of the Botanicals

Daisies twirl with daffodil,
Arm in arm, they spin at will.
Giggling leaves and roots unite,
Under the rays of warm sunlight.

Cacti join in with a shrug,
While vines embrace in a hug.
Each plant's a comical star,
In this botanical bazaar.

Layered Horizons

Layer upon layer, quite absurd,
Vegetables form a silly herd.
Potatoes rolling in delight,
Carrots dancing through the night.

Zucchinis leap and do their spin,
Bouncing peas, let the fun begin!
In horizons rich with cheer,
Nature's laughter draws us near.

From Soil to Sky

In the ground where it started,
Little sprouts peek with glee,
They twist and shout like dancers,
Determined to be free.

They stretch up tall like giants,
With dreams of reaching clouds,
Just one step at a time,
They cheer, oh so loud!

But then comes the wind's giggle,
It bends them left and right,
They wobble and they wobble,
Making quite a sight!

And as they rise to greet Sun,
They wave their leaves so bright,
With laughter in their laughter,
They reach for sheer delight.

A Tangle of Life

In a garden filled with chaos,
The plants begin to dance,
One leaf stepped on another,
They all just love this chance.

"I'm not a weed!" shouts Clover,
"I'm dressed in green so neat!"
But tangled in a mishmash,
They form a jangled fleet.

Vines wrap around each other,
Like friends that love to hug,
They giggle in the sunlight,
Not a single one to shrug.

Through thorns and big wide petals,
They chirp a merry tune,
In this tangled garden glory,
They cheer beneath the Moon!

The Unraveling Vine

There once was a sly little vine,
Who thought it wise to entwine,
Around a big old tree trunk,
Making sure it looked fine.

But as it climbed up the bark,
It tangled its leaves and tail,
Each twist was quite amusing,
A very comical trail.

"Oh dear, I'm quite a pickle!",
The vine declared with a grin,
"If I twist just a bit more,
I might fall, oh where to begin?"

With a chuckle from the branches,
The tree looked down and spoke,
"Just enjoy your goofy journey,
It's all a part of the joke!"

Seedlings in the Breeze

Little seedlings on the ground,
Are taking in the show,
With tiny roots, they giggle,
As the funny winds do blow.

They sway like dancers, jumping,
"Oh look! A butterfly!"
With dreams of taking flight,
They all begin to sigh.

Suddenly comes a raindrop,
They squeal with playful screams,
"We're growing up so quickly,
I can't believe our dreams!"

With features all a-poppin',
And giggles loud and clear,
These seedlings chase the windy breeze,
With joy and silly cheer!

Journey Through Green

In the depths of a leafy maze,
I tripped on a branch, in quite a daze.
The squirrels laughed, oh what a sight,
As I stumbled and tumbled, with all my might.

A rabbit winked, in his cool little hat,
Said, "Watch your step, dear human! Look at that!"
With every twist, the trees would wave,
As nature giggled, my path they brave.

The ferns whispered jokes, quite absurd,
While I fumbled for balance, feeling so blurred.
A dandelion danced, with seeds on a breeze,
Spreading laughter like pollen, if you please!

I chortled with ivy, all tangled and funny,
As I bumped a big oak, "Call me a honey!"
In this forest so wild, with hues ever bright,
Every mistake brought pure delight.

Blossoms of Tomorrow

In a garden of blooms, with color so bold,
The flowers sang songs, stories untold.
A daisy declared, "I'm queen for a day!"
While tulips giggled, in their own little way.

A sunflower spun, head held up high,
Challenging bees to a race through the sky.
"All this pollen, what a tasty snack!
With a buzz and a buzz, they all flew back!"

The lilacs waved, in the midday cheer,
"I'll bloom through the autumn, let's give a cheer!"
But a tired old rose said, "Not so fast!
I'll be the one here, pretending to last!"

Together they chuckled, a chorus of glee,
In this patch of color, so wild and free.
The future looked bright, with laughter in tow,
As blossoms of tomorrow began to glow.

Veins of the Forest

In the veins of the forest, where shadows play,
Lived creatures who danced in a quirky ballet.
A tortoise twirled, in a top hat so slick,
While a raccoon juggled, oh what a trick!

The roots whispered secrets, old as the trees,
While moss laughed along with the rustling leaves.
Beneath the green light, squirrels would chat,
"I think I just saw a dancing acrobat!"

The ferns cracked jokes about their big fronds,
While fireflies twinkled like little diamonds.
In the heart of the woods, where the humor grows loud,
The trees wore smiles, standing tall and proud.

With every odd sound, the creatures would cheer,
Celebrating the joy that was always near.
So dance through the veins, let your spirit roam,
In this forest of laughter, you're never alone.

Intertwined Paths

On twisted trails, where laughter collides,
The flowers invite with their colorful hides.
"Take a left at the giggle, and right at the cheer,"
Said a bumblebee buzzing, with nothing to fear.

The vines intertwined, telling tales of old,
Of mischief and fun, of brave hearts bold.
As I wandered the paths, a frog jumped in sight,
"Jump if you dare, do it with all your might!"

A hedgehog offered directions, but spun in a whirl,
"Oops! That's my tail, care for a twirl?"
While laughter erupted from the branches above,
In this woodland maze, it was all about love.

So tread on these trails, let the joy intertwine,
With friendly critters, you'll surely feel fine.
For in every path taken, a chuckle you'll find,
In the intertwining woods, humor's one of a kind.

The Pulse of Progress

In the garden, plants all prance,
Each leaf is trying for a chance.
They sway and giggle in the breeze,
While ants march on as if to tease.

A flower shouts with all its might,
"Look at me! I'm quite a sight!"
But the weeds chuckle, oh so sly,
"We love to bloom, but we just lie!"

The birch tree thinks it's really tall,
While daisies whisper, "Not at all!"
The dandelions blow their seeds,
"We're winning here! Come join our leads!"

In the soil, the worms all dance,
Digging deep, they take a chance.
Each squirm a giggle, quite the jest,
In this garden, we're all blessed.

Nature's Interludes

The squirrels play tag, they dash and dart,
Chasing shadows, a wild art.
While mushrooms giggle, looking round,
At the snap of twigs, a silly sound.

A butterfly lands, it's quite the flirt,
While daisies blush, they're quite the spurt.
"We bloom with pride!" the tulips boast,
As bees hum tunes, they're quite the host.

The stream gurgles, making a joke,
A rock replies, "I'm no mere bloke!"
With laughter rippling down the lane,
The creatures join, oh what a gain!

In nature's play, we take a role,
From munching rabbits to the pole.
With every chuckle, our spirits rise,
In every nook, surprise supplies.

Shaping the Roots

In the soil, the secrets grow,
With little critters running to and fro.
Each beetle wears a tiny hat,
While worms converse and tip their spat.

The cabbage rolls with laughter loud,
While onions hide beneath a shroud.
Carrots giggle, dancing below,
As rows of veggies steal the show.

"Hey, look at me!" the radish sings,
As seedlings sprout on hopeful wings.
The sunbeams play, a warm embrace,
In this humble, lively space.

Each root entwines like pals on fun,
In the garden's waltz, they all have won.
A riot of greens, a bouncing band,
Together they rise, hand in hand.

The Whispering Woods

In the woods, the trees exchange a laugh,
"I'm taller!" one boasts by half.
The saplings giggle, swaying small,
"You'll see us grow, we'll soon stand tall!"

The bushes gossip, sharing news,
While ivy climbs, it's got the blues.
"I'll wrap around!" the vines all tease,
As twigs snap back, blowing in the breeze.

A squirrel chimes in with a joke or two,
"I've seen a bird that lost its shoe!"
With every cackle, leaves start to shake,
In this forest, joy's no mistake.

Whispers of laughter weave through the air,
In nature's world, there's fun to spare.
The woods alive, with the sound of cheer,
In every corner, friendship is near.

Between Earth and Air

In the garden, plants giggle,
As they stretch their leaves high.
Worms waltz beneath the soil,
While butterflies flit by.

A tomato wore a grin,
As it ripened in the sun.
"Ketchup's just around the bend!"
Said the mustard, full of fun.

Cucumbers play hide-and-seek,
Peeking from their leafy lair.
Watching garden gnomes on guard,
Suspicious of their stare.

So here's to nature's folly,
With every twist and turn.
The laughter of the seedlings,
In the age-old art we learn.

Flourish and Fade

Roses wear their finest hats,
While daisies play tag nearby.
In the pot, a silly cactus,
Says, "I'll try to say hi!"

The sunflowers take selfies,
With bumblebees as guests.
"Say cheese," they buzz, all clumsy,
Just hoping for the best.

But not all plants are fashion stars,
Some prefer the plain.
The weeds laugh and roll their eyes,
In their wild, unkempt reign.

Life's a dance of bloom and droop,
Where laughter hides and waits.
The circle of the garden's life,
Is a party at the gates.

Life in a Whisper

Underneath the leafy hugs,
The gossip flows like streams.
The carrots tell the radishes,
About their secret dreams.

A pear tree leans in closer,
"I had the juiciest night!"
While a berry blushes crimson,
Embarrassed by its plight.

Napping naps of dandelions,
Tickle in the breeze.
Frogs croak their raucous songs,
Trying hard to tease.

A world of quiet chatter,
In nature's silly show.
Whispers dance on roots and branches,
Setting laughter all aglow.

The Canvas of the Canopy

A squirrel paints with acorns,
On branches high and bright.
While leaves drop down like laughter,
In a golden, fluttering flight.

The birds critique his artwork,
With tweets that fill the air.
"More color on the edges!"
"Make sure you blend with flair!"

The trees sway in agreement,
Joining in the fun.
"Let's move our limbs a little,
To help the shadows run!"

In this whimsical gallery,
Nature's artists play and roam.
Each season adds a layer,
Creating a leafy home.

Roots of Resilience

In the garden, we all stand tall,
Roots gripping tightly, that's the call.
Even when storms start to brew,
We dance with the rain, just me and you.

With mud on our shoes and weeds in sight,
We laugh with the bugs that come for a bite.
Holding our ground, it's quite a task,
Yet here we are, no need to ask.

Through trials and fuss, we manage to thrive,
Giggling with daisies, oh, how we strive!
Though some may stumble, we never fall,
Our roots are strong, we weather it all.

Petals in the Wind

Blown about like a playful kite,
Petals twirl, oh what a sight!
In the breeze, they sway and spin,
A raucous dance, let the fun begin!

Some rest on noses, others on hats,
Tickling toes like silly little brats.
A butterfly chorus joins the show,
All the while, the daisies glow.

Each petal giggles as it takes flight,
Chasing the sun, pure delight.
From one flower to another they race,
In this wild and whimsical space!

Budding Dreams

In the garden, ideas start to sprout,
Tiny green whispers, without a doubt.
With a sprinkle of laughter, they reach for the sky,
Like silly little sprouts, oh my, oh my!

Each dream a budding flower, bright and new,
A wobbly stem, what will it do?
With sunshine and giggles, they rise and shine,
A patchwork of hopes, oh so divine!

Sometimes they trip, or they might just sway,
But that's part of the fun, come what may.
So let's plant our dreams, let's make 'em beam,
In this playful garden, we'll all scheme!

Branches of Hope

Up high they stretch, on a mischievous spree,
Branches jive, well, just wait and see!
They tickle the clouds and scratch at the moon,
Swaying like dancers, in a happy tune.

With laughter and leaves, they swing from the bough,
"Hang on tight! It's a wild ride now!"
Each branch a story, a joke to be told,
Woven in laughter, like threads of gold.

As the sun dips low, their shadows grow long,
Echoing giggles, a playful song.
Together they giggle, in moonlight they gleam,
Branches of hope, living the dream!

Ascending Dreams

In a garden high up on a beam,
A squirrel tried to fly and scream.
He tied up his nuts like a little kite,
But acorns just don't take flight.

A dandelion danced with a breeze,
While a snail still pondered its fees.
"Who knew grass could be so profound?"
The worms laughed hard, rolling around.

The flowers wore hats made of soup,
While bees formed a lazy, buzzing group.
They decided to throw a big feast,
With petals for plates and pollen at least.

Yet amidst the fun, a wise old tree,
Said, "Time to settle; come up for tea!"
Then they all paused, just like in a dream,
And giggled along with the sun's own beam.

The Nature of Connection

A vine tried to hug a garden gate,
But it pulled too hard and said, "Wait!"
A crabapple laughed, rolling on the floor,
"You missed! It's not that kind of door!"

Grasshoppers played hopscotch on the path,
While daisies burst out in cheerful laugh.
"Can tulips join? We want to dance!"
"But your twirls look more like a prance!"

The potting soil told all the jokes,
As the carrots giggled with earthy folks.
A tomato blushed redder than a peach,
"Let's plant ideas! They're within reach!"

So roots intertwined, and saplings met,
A fiesta of greens without a fret.
Nature's connection, a feathery twist,
For every sprout knew it couldn't resist.

Tendrils of Hope

A cucumber climbed up a wooden chair,
And gave the old cat quite a scare.
"Don't use my leg as your little spree,"
Cried the cat who just wanted her tea!

Potatoes went rolling, having a ball,
Yelling, "We're tubers! We rule this hall!"
They formed a parade, all covered in dirt,
With radishes red, and beets wearing shirts.

The garlic held dreams of a grand ballet,
As onions just cried, "We won't let 'em stay!"
So they flicked their green tops, a wild array,
While sprouts danced merrily, come what may.

Then a witty grape sang a funny tune,
While sunshine giggled, bright as the moon.
With all of their antics, they'd rise and joke,
In the garden of dreams, they oftentimes spoke.

In the Garden of Solitude

In solitude sat a cucumber sage,
Worrying much about the next stage.
"I'd like to chat with a carrot or two,
But they're busy growing, who even knew?"

A lonely radish sighed with despair,
"In this vast garden, does anyone care?"
Just then a lazy snail slithered by,
"Cheer up! We have clouds and the sky!"

"The bees might buzz by with their gossip,"
Said the lettuce, who couldn't quite stop it.
"A party could sprout on a leafy green isle,
Let's pull on our roots and dance for a while!"

So the garden transformed into laughter and cheer,
With every plant sharing something sincere.
In the silence once felt, now joy intertwined,
For even alone, connection you'll find.

Nature's Tapestry Unfolds

In the garden, plants wear hats,
Daisies whisper to lazy cats.
Crickets dance in a slapstick show,
As beetles race, putting on a faux glow.

The trees gossip about the sun,
While squirrels call it a day done.
Frogs hop by in a comical leap,
While worms wiggle, making all giggle and peep.

Butterflies flirt and tickle the breeze,
While ants march on with such great ease.
Peeking daisies play peek-a-boo,
While grandpa oak snores, old but true.

In this patch of laughter, joy, and cheer,
Nature's humor is loud and clear.
Each bloom a chuckle, each green a grin,
In this playful realm, we all fit in.

The Language of Green

Vines argue about who climbs best,
While ferns take naps without a quest.
A cactus grins and tries to tease,
"I'm prickly, but you're so unease!"

Grasshoppers chirp in a symphony,
While ladybugs plot a mini spree.
Rabbits prance in funky shoes,
As flowers gossip of love and ruse.

A sunflower winks at a passing bee,
While daisies stomp their roots in glee.
"Who will dance when the rain descends?"
In green's chatter, fun never ends.

Whispers of nature tickle the air,
Each leaf a joke, none are rare.
With every rustle, the green world beams,
In a giggling garden, nothing's what it seems.

Budding Promises

Tiny sprouts poke their heads with flair,
Promising blooms, with laughter to share.
A bud pops open and says, "Look at me!"
While ants cheer, as happy as can be.

Petals twirl in a dance so slick,
While bees hum along, giving a kick.
"Who will bloom first?" the tulips ask,
While daisies giggle at their small task.

A daffodil bows, full of conceit,
"Can you make me a crown? I'm so sweet!"
With each bud bursting, joy takes a leap,
Nature's whimsy is a treasure to keep.

The garden's alive with a jolly jest,
Each bloom a punchline, sunshine's best.
In nature's kingdom, laughter's the scheme,
Blooming joyfully, a shared happy dream.

Echoes of the Earth

The ground chuckles, shaking with glee,
As worms perform their wiggle spree.
"Who can wriggle the fastest?" they tease,
While mosses sigh in whispers with ease.

Rocks sit back, with wisdom to lend,
"Life's a jest, my leafy friend!"
The breeze carries tales of laughter and fun,
As petals clap when a new day's begun.

Rivers giggle, splashing along,
Playing tunes of bubbly song.
"Catch me if you can!" they giggle and sigh,
While pebbles chuckle as they lie dry.

Echoes of nature in joyful refrain,
Create a canvas of humor not plain.
From roots to the sky, all share the mirth,
In every corner, the echoes of Earth.

The Quiet Emergence

In the garden's calm embrace,
Seeds have decided to join the race.
Peeking out with silly glee,
They're shouting, "Look, it's party time! See?"

A tiny sprout just lost its hat,
It tripped on roots while chasing a rat.
With dirt on its nose, it can't take a stand,
"Who knew that growing could be so grand?"

Butterflies giggle, watching the show,
As daisies dance with a wobbly flow.
They whisper to tulips in shades of pink,
"Let's grow a floor for a garden drink!"

So here they come, a jolly band,
Floppy leaves giving each other a hand.
The quiet emergence has turned quite loud,
With laughter and joy, they're making a crowd.

Climbing Towards the Light

A little vine with a lofty goal,
Decided to climb, oh what a stroll!
It slipped on dew, then slipped on cheer,
"Who knew climbing could tickle the ear?"

Beneath the sun, it wobbled wide,
Chasing rays with a froggy stride.
Some say it's seeking a sunbeam snack,
While others shout, "Hey! Don't look back!"

Caterpillars cheer, "You can do this, friend!"
As laughter among the leaves does blend.
"Just watch your step or you might fall,
But hey, who needs balance when having a ball?"

So up it goes, with a silly sway,
Chasing the light in a funny way.
With a twist and a turn, it claims its throne,
Climbing towards joy, never alone.

Nature's Secret Gardener

There's a gardener, quiet as a mouse,
Whispering secrets throughout the house.
With mud on its boots and a grin so wide,
It tends to the plants that hug and hide.

A daisy asked, "What's the trick, oh wise?"
The gardener sighed, "It's all in the surprise!"
"Just sprinkle some giggles, add laughter's delight,
And the flowers will bloom like stars in the night!"

Tulips danced, swaying from side to side,
As the gardener tossed sprinkles with pride.
"Water with fun, and soon you'll delight,
Be ready to burst out in colors so bright!"

So under the sun, the plants all cheered,
For the secret gardener they so revered.
With a wink and a nod, it tiptoed away,
Leaving behind a garden at play!

Whispers in the Wild

In the wild where whispers roam,
A cactus told a joke to a gnome.
"Why did the flower blush, oh my?"
It giggled soft, as butterflies fly.

The trees laughed, swaying left and right,
As squirrels held a dance party, what a sight!
"Gather 'round, don't be shy or meek,
Let's hear the tales of every cheek!"

A fern chimed in, "I'm feeling spry!"
With fronds dancing like stars in the sky.
"Life's a giggle, a playful trend,
So let's make memories till the end!"

From roots to branches, the laughter soared,
In whispers and giggles, nature adored.
So next time you wander where wild things abide,
Remember the joy that nature won't hide.

Tangles of Tenacity

In a garden so wild, I found my way,
Weaving through weeds that love to play.
A twist here, a knot there, oh what a sight,
Dancing with nature, it's pure delight!

With tangled roots and blooms askew,
I laughed at the chaos, how 'bout you?
Each petal a giggle, each thorn a joke,
In the mess of the green, I'm never broke!

My friends all ask, 'Why so unkempt?'
I shrug and I say, 'It's nature's attempt!'
With sun on my face, and dirt on my knees,
I live for the laughter, and the buzzing bees!

So here's to the tangles where mischief thrives,
In this jumbled patch, oh, joy arrives!
With snickers of blooms and chuckles of grass,
My garden's a party—come join en masse!

Fragments of Life

Life's a puzzle made of petals bright,
Chasing sunshine, oh what a sight!
With stitches of laughter, stitches of tears,
Each piece tells a story through all of the years.

A leaf flutters down, a dance with the breeze,
Silly little moments that aim to please.
Dandelion wishes float high in the air,
While crickets debate on the best way to share.

In gardens of chaos, I sift through the mess,
With humor, I find that life can't be less.
Every petal, every leaf, a fragment to see,
Reminding me always to just let it be.

So I gather these moments, both funny and wise,
Crafting a life that's a sweet surprise.
With each little fragment, a giggle or cheer,
Fragments of life—what a joy to hold dear!

Gardens of Reflection

In a patch of green, I took a seat,
Among the flowers, so absurdly sweet.
They whispered secrets in giggling tones,
While I pondered life with the bees and stones.

A sunflower grins, with petals so wide,
As the daisy plays hide and seek with pride.
I chuckle and ponder, am I just as bright?
Or simply a shadow in the waning light?

The nettles are prickly, but boy, do they shine,
With their spunky humor, they don't toe the line.
Reflection grows in this garden of mine,
With laughter and giggles, I feel so divine!

So let's stroll and ponder, with nature as muse,
In gardens of reflection, we can't lose!
With smiles all around, let's take a chance,
To dance in the flowers, and laugh as they prance!

The Lullaby of Leaves

In the trees above, a melody plays,
Each leaf dancing gently, caught in the haze.
With rustles and whispers, they sing me to sleep,
As I dream of the laughter that nature's so deep.

A breeze like a giggle flutters on by,
While squirrels plot jokes under the sky.
A symphony of chuckles surrounds my rest,
In the arms of the branches, I'm surely blessed.

The chorus of crickets backs up the trees,
Singing songs of the garden, what joy and what ease!
While shadows are dancing, and fireflies play,
It's a lullaby of leaves at the end of the day.

So lay down your worries, hear nature's embrace,
With humor and heart, let it all fall in place.
In the lullaby of leaves, we weave dreams and cheer,
As the night wraps us softly, there's nothing to fear!

Bindings of the Wild

In the thicket, a squirrel prances,
Chasing shadows, taking chances.
The vines twist like they play a game,
Raccoons plot, oh what a shame!

A rabbit hops with grace and flair,
Climbs a tree to savor air.
But who needs grass when you can bounce,
Worms just watch, they can't announce!

The bushes whisper funny tales,
Of hedgehogs in tiny pails.
While owls chuckle, wise and sly,
At the antics of the shy.

Each creature dances, wild and free,
In this fun-filled jubilee.
Nature's laugh is loud and clear,
In this wild, we shed a tear!

Nature's Geometry

In circles round, the daisies spin,
While bees buzz by, they wear a grin.
The cactus sports a pointy hat,
As lizards tease the nearby cat.

Leaves in triangles wave and sway,
Whilst ants parade in a conga way.
A snail breaks free from its slow show,
And reveals a dance we all want to know!

The mushrooms giggle, small and wise,
As woodpeckers tap with a surprise.
They count their steps, in lines so neat,
While crickets strum a funky beat.

With patterns bright, nature's art,
Unites all beasts, plays every part.
In shapes and forms, they leap and run,
For laughter shared is the greatest fun!

Blooms of Resilience

Out of cracks, flowers boldly sprout,
With colors shouting, there's no doubt!
A dandelion in the concrete,
Yells, "Take that!" with much conceit.

While daisies scheme a grand parade,
To outshine weeds, a light charade.
Petals waving, full of zest,
They challenge roses to the test!

In the rain, a cheery bloom,
Shows off glories in nature's room.
With hearty laughs, they quip and jest,
Each trying to be the fanciest guest.

Though seasons change, they never fret,
For every bud knows no regret.
With roots so deep, they'll take a stand,
Blooming bright in every land!

Under the Canopy

Under branches, the fun begins,
Where squirrels wear their acorn pins.
The shadows play a sneaky game,
While mushrooms cheer, they stake their claim.

A parrot squawks a silly joke,
As turtles laugh in their slow poke.
With whispers soft, the ferns all say,
"Join our dance, just for today!"

The sunbeams poke through leafy greens,
Illuminating all the scenes.
A breeze then tickles, sets us free,
As nature wraps us joyfully!

Under the canopy, joy is found,
With laughter echoing all around.
Come join the fun, don't miss the cue,
For nature's laughs are just for you!

In the Thicket of Thorns

In the garden, thorns do prance,
They poke and prod, not giving a chance.
The roses laugh, growing with flair,
While the thorns plot schemes, unaware of repair.

A cheeky fern waves with glee,
"Look at the chaos, come dance with me!"
With prickles and giggles, they twirl and spin,
In the patch of thorns, where mischief begins.

The daisies snicker, their petals so bright,
As the thistles grumble, barred from the light.
Yet all together, they form quite a show,
A zany bouquet in a spiky tableau.

So tiptoe through thorns, be wary and free,
In their pointy playground where laughter runs free.
Embrace the wild and enjoy the plight,
For even the prickly can bring sheer delight.

Pathways of the Bloom

In a vibrant field of colors so grand,
The flowers whisper, hand in hand.
"Step this way!" a tulip calls,
But watch your feet! They'll trip and fall!

Dandelions chuckle, their seeds take flight,
While daisies giggle in pure delight.
"We're on a journey, join our parade!"
With each little petal, new paths are laid.

The poppies prance, their skirts a sway,
"Come frolic with us, let's play all day!"
Through winding trails of green and bloom,
They twist and twirl, dispelling the gloom.

In this laughter where petals collide,
Each bloom a companion on a joyride.
With colors and chuckles, forever they share,
In the merry meadow, there's always a flare.

Vital Signs of Green

In the jungle, green and bright,
Leaves wear glasses, a comical sight.
"Find the sun!" they joke with vibrant cheer,
While the ferns whisper, "Don't stay too near!"

The waddling weeds do a dance on the floor,
Spinning and twirling, they beg for encore.
"Vital signs?" croaks the moss on a log,
"Only if you check my mood, don't be a cog!"

Cacti play cards, sharp but quite sly,
Trading their secrets, as breezes float by.
"Winning hand!" laughs the leafy brigade,
In this jungle of greens, mischief is made.

So dance through the greenery, let laughter flow,
From the tips of the leaves to the roots down below.
Each chuckle and giggle, a sign of their health,
In the wild, vibrant world where joy is their wealth.

The Layers of Life

Peel back the layers, what do we find?
A world full of whimsy, no need to unwind.
Each petal a story, each leaf a song,
In the garden of humor, nothing feels wrong.

From roots that burble, to stems that sway,
The laughter of life has a playful way.
"Look at my layers!" a bulb does insist,
But it's the laughter that truly persists.

The soil grumbles softly, a wise little sage,
"In every funny turn, I'm quite the stage!"
As worms slither past, with winks in their eyes,
In this layered drama, laughter never dies.

So dig a bit deeper, embrace each delight,
In the layers of life, everything's light.
With giggles and chuckles, it's all intertwined,
Embrace all the layers, the fun you will find.

The Sway of the Wild

In the jungle, plants do dance,
Their leaves do twirl and prance.
A parrot joins in, without a care,
Laughing loudly, it's quite a scare.

The vines are tangled, a silly sight,
Twirling like dancers, oh what a fright!
Frogs are croaking in rhythm, too,
As if saying, "Look at me, woo-hoo!"

Grasshoppers jump to the beat,
Creating chaos, oh what a feat!
The trees are swaying, feeling fine,
Even the cactus sways in line!

So in the wild, jokes abound,
Nature's humor is all around.
With every shake and shimmy they show,
The fun of life in their leafy glow.

Tendrils of Time

Time slips by like a curling vine,
Twisting round as nature's sign.
A squirrel races to catch a nut,
Tripping on roots—oh, what a rut!

The clock ticks slow, but leaves fly fast,
Moments linger, yet vanish at last.
A worm pokes out with a giggle and grin,
"Hey buddy, mind if I join in?"

Days uncoil like a playful spring,
Chasing shadows, what jests they bring!
When the moon laughs, and the stars play tag,
You can't help but feel a little brag.

So spin and twist, let the laughter climb,
Through the tangled days, and the vines of time.
Life's a comedy, with silly rhymes,
In the garden's embrace, we find our chimes.

A Green Odyssey

On a quest through the jungle bright,
Where leaves all shimmer in sunlight.
A raccoon wears a hat made of grass,
Exclaims, "Watch out! Here comes a sass!"

Beneath the ferns, a snail takes flight,
Not really, he's just modeling his might.
"I'm speedy!" he shouts, though going quite slow,
All the critters just laugh, "Look at him go!"

The sunflowers gossip, with faces so wide,
Sharing tall tales of a plant-like tide.
While daisies dance in their dainty way,
Twisting and twirling, come join the play!

Embarking on this leafy spree,
Every day brings mystery.
A journey full of chuckles, delight,
In this green amusement, we take flight!

Blossoms of Yesterday

Once blooming petals whispered humor,
Giggling softly—what a rumor!
"I saw a bee in a silly hat,
Buzzing loudly, oh imagine that!"

In the garden, tales take flight,
Of flowers fighting for the light.
A tulip claimed, "I'm the fairest here!"
While daisies chuckle, "Oh my dear!"

Time trips over like a clumsy bug,
Tickling plants with a playful tug.
The roses blush, but join in the jest,
"Nature's a joke, we're all the best!"

So come and wander through yesterday's blooms,
Find laughter hiding in nature's rooms.
With every twist, and each little bend,
The garden whispers, "Life's a funny friend!"

The Dance of the Seasons

Spring skipped in with daisies bright,
Summer tripped on its own sunlight.
Fall decided to roll and tumble,
Winter laughed, while the other seasons fumbled.

They twirled through fields, so carefree,
Slipped on leaves with such glee.
Chasing shadows, they made a scene,
As winter grinned, looking so mean!

"Who stole my snow?" winter did shout,
"Just let me win, or I'll pout!"
Seasons chuckled, playing their game,
Each one trying to claim the fame!

So they dance on, day by day,
With funny slips and wild ballet.
A seasonal show, a charming jest,
In nature's theater, they are the best!

Underneath the Canopy

Under leaves where the critters play,
Squirrels party, hip hip hooray!
Rabbits hop and do a jig,
While ants march strong, oh so big!

"Who brought the snacks?" a birdie whines,
"We need some seeds to fuel our lines!"
The mossy floor's a dance hall floor,
With fungi shuffling, wanting more!

A beetle beats a drum of clay,
While fireflies flash to light the way.
Cockroaches wiggle with flair so bold,
As nature's disco unfolds, uncontrolled!

The canopy cracks with laughter bright,
Every creature mingling, what a sight!
In this leafy club, they sing and cheer,
Nature's own gathering, oh so dear!

Revelations in Bloom

In the garden where petals peek,
Daisies gossip and roses speak.
"Who's got the best color?" they tease,
While tulips nod in the soft breeze.

A sunflower towers, waving hello,
"Hey little buds, come join the show!"
Laughter erupts from their leafy hearts,
As bees buzz by with their sweet arts.

"Stop pushing me, you thorny brat!"
A little bloom in a spat is caught.
The violets giggle and blush with mirth,
Nature's bloomers know their worth!

Petals ruffled, they sway and bend,
Sharing secrets, as friends will mend.
In this patch, the jokes are bright,
Revelations sprout in delight!

Threads of Nature

In the web of life, all stitches align,
Worms weave tales as they dine.
Spiders spin stories, round and round,
While caterpillars crawl, looking quite profound.

"Need a hand? I'm all knotted!"
A clumsy bug exclaimed, rather sotted.
"Don't pull so hard, you'll ruin the fun!"
With wobbly threads, they came undone.

Bees busy buzzing, stitching the air,
With golden threads, they really care.
Butterflies flutter, their colors grand,
In this funny tale of nature's band!

So gather 'round, in this fabric of glee,
Every stitch tells a tale, just wait and see!
Threads of nature, in laughter entwined,
Oh, what a tapestry of a different kind!

The Secret Life of Roots

In the dark where whispers grow,
The roots have secrets, don't you know?
They gossip late, they giggle tight,
About the flowers in the light.

They plan escapades, oh what a scene,
With tiny worms, they plot so keen.
A rendezvous at half past four,
Underneath the soil's grand door.

They prank the weeds, tie them in knots,
Dance with beetles, share funny spots.
Laughter echoes through the ground,
In their world, joy does abound.

So if you see a dancing sprout,
Just know the roots are sprouting out!
With laughter shared, they sway and bend,
The secret life that knows no end.

Flourishing in Chaos

In the garden, crazy and wild,
Life erupts like a playful child.
Tulips trip on daisies' toes,
While sunflowers practice silly poses.

The ivy competes in a tangled race,
Climbing higher with a goofy face.
Every petal tries to outshine,
As ladybugs start to dine on wine.

Even the grasses have their say,
With windy dances, come what may.
Bumblebees buzz in acrobatic flight,
In this fun-filled, chaotic delight.

All things blooming, naught but a jest,
In the chaos, they find their best.
Together, they laugh without a care,
Nature's spectacle, a comic affair.

Enchanted Understory

Beneath the trees, a world unfolds,
Where mushrooms wear hats, joyfully bold.
The ferns like to twirl in the breeze,
Making TikTok dances with ease.

Squirrels throw parties with acorn treats,
Inviting the foxes for fancy eats.
While rabbits tell tales of daring feats,
In shadows where excitement beats.

The shadows giggle, inclining to sway,
To the rhythm of critters that jump and play.
A hidden realm of whimsical fun,
Where laughter mingles under the sun.

In this understory of curious tales,
Everyone sings and no one fails.
Join the laughter, come take a chance,
In this magical, merry dance.

The Fabric of Flora

A tapestry woven from colors bright,
Where petals hang out and bask in light.
With threads of green and strokes of gold,
Nature's comedy, a sight to behold.

The daisies compete for the sun's sweet kiss,
While tulips flip their petals with bliss.
Each bloom tells a joke and shares a grin,
In this vibrant world, let the fun begin.

Vines swing like kids on swings so high,
While clouds float by with a giggly sigh.
Every leaf knows how to partake,
In the frolic of laughter, the joy they make.

So here in the garden, a laugh you'll find,
In nature's laughter, we're all entwined.
The fabric of flora, a patchwork dream,
Woven together, we dance and beam.

From Seed to Bloom

A little seed fell from a tree,
It rolled away, quite happily.
"I'll bloom like flowers on a hill,"
But first, a worm slipped in for a thrill.

Sunshine beamed, rain sang its tune,
But instead of petals, it grew a raccoon!
"Hey, that's not meant to happen, you see!"
Raccoon just smiled, "I'm part of the spree!"

They danced and sang, quite out of tune,
Making friends with a big, fat balloon.
Together they twirled with joy and glee,
Who knew a seed could host a party spree?

At last, it bloomed, but here's the jest,
A raccoon dress, and it's looking its best!
"From sprout to bloom, it's all kinds of fun,"
Giggles and laughter, and they're not yet done!

The Journey Within

Deep in the soil, a seed began,
Dreamt of the day to be a great plan.
"I'll dig my way to the sky so high!"
But ended up under a passing pie.

A squirrel looked down, chuckling right quick,
"Your journey's a mess! Want to try a trick?"
The seed rolled and tumbled, oh what a sight,
Out popped a sprout with a grin so bright.

They played tag with roots, chased bugs that zoom,
"What a funny home," they exclaimed with boom.
"Let's reach for the clouds and dodge all the birds,"
But tripping on worms, they forgot their words.

The journey was wild, a right comedy,
With laughs from the leaves, full of glee.
A green little sprout, not quite what was planned,
But oh, how it danced in its quirky land!

Verdant Chronicles

In a garden alive with giggles and hue,
A daring sprout said, "Look at me, too!"
I'll grow so tall, reach the sun on high,
But got tangled up in a bright blue tie.

A ladybug laughed, rolling with glee,
"Come join our dance, let's make history!"
But a gust of wind brought a ruckus so loud,
The sprout lost its tie, and it danced like a cloud.

Flower friends joined, with wigs made of grass,
All twirling about, like they had too much sass.
"Let's form a band, our roots keep the beat!"
But stumbled on rocks, tripping over their feet.

So the verdant crew laughed till the night,
With giggly moonbeams, so sparkly and bright.
The chronicles told of their whimsical strife,
In a dance of the garden, such a silly life!

The Pulse of the Forest

In the heart of the woods, where laughter runs free,
A tiny plant tried to shout, "Look at me!"
But all it could manage was a squeaky "Hi!"
As birds laughed aloud, buzzing close by.

The squirrels held meetings with nuts stacked so high,
"How to support our friend who's too shy?"
With acorn hats and some berries for flair,
They dressed up the plant, now brave with their dare.

Then came a deer, with a bounce and a hop,
"Join us in prancing; we'll never stop!"
But tangled in vines, the shy plant exclaimed,
"Why is this fun if I'm still unnamed?"

They roared with laughter, gave it a crown,
"You're the Forest King, wear this leafy gown!"
So it twerked with the trees, danced where it may,
In the pulse of the forest, where silliness stays!

The Weaving of Seasons

Leaves in a bustle, rustling about,
Squirrels in knickers, running about.
Sunshine is giggling, clouds start to dance,
Nature's parade gets a silly romance.

Breezes are ticklish, whispering jokes,
Flowers all chuckling, wearing their cloaks.
Rain starts to juggle, puddles are wide,
The world's a stage—come join for a ride!

Caterpillars clapping, butterflies soar,
Geese in tuxedos, what's the encore?
All the trees swaying, knees knocking too,
In the season's circus, there's laughter anew.

So grab your umbrella, come laugh in the sun,
In this splendid garden, life's just begun!

Patterns in the Blades

Grass blades are waving, making a scene,
Competing for fun, in colors of green.
A worm in a bowtie, gives a grand bow,
While ants march in sync—they steal the show now.

Dandelions giggle, fluffing their crowns,
As bees wear top hats, buzzing in towns.
Each blade whispers secrets, in tales that they weave,
Of knock-knock jokes told, 'round the conifer leaves.

Spiders spin laughter, tangled with tricks,
With webs made of giggles, and numberless flicks.
The daisies do cha-cha, beneath the bright sun,
While grasshoppers hop, claiming they're on the run!

In patterns of folly, life's rhythm is grand,
Join the fun garden party—take a strong stand!

Growth Rings of Time

Each year's a new pancake, flipped with a grin,
Layers of laughter, where does it begin?
Old trees tell tales, with faces of glee,
Wrapping up moments, for you and for me.

Bark cracks with laughter, stretching for miles,
Rings of bright memories, layered with smiles.
Time's silly dance, on the woodland floor,
Reminds us that laughter is what we're here for.

Branches are reaching, high fives in the breeze,
Fruits of the seasons, like sunshine with cheese.
Each cut and each curve, tells a funny old tale,
Of raucous adventures, in the sweet leafy veil.

So tally up giggles, and sprinkle faux pine,
For growth is much better, when laughter aligns!

Echoes in the Garden

Whispers of flowers, tickling the air,
Each petal a giggle, without a care.
Mud pies are laughing, splashing about,
In the echoing garden, can you hear the shout?

Beetles on tricycles, racing a snail,
With a wink and a nudge, they're off on their trail.
Silly old frogs, croaking funny tunes,
Under the watch of the chuckling moons.

Butterflies chuckle, making new friends,
In the symphony of laughter, where joy never ends.
The sun's on a swing, all day it rocks,
While shadows are playing with colorful socks.

In this joyful haven, so bright and so free,
Echoes of laughter, live here—come and see!

Echoes of Roots

In a garden where giggles sprout,
A worm wiggled, shaking about.
It tickled a flower, who burst into glee,
Saying, "Dance on my petals, you silly old flea!"

Nests of ants marched in a line,
Stomped on a beetle, oh how divine!
"Excuse me!" it shouted, "That's quite the parade!"
But the ants just laughed, their dance never swayed.

A cactus wore shades, trying hard to be cool,
But all he got was the title of fool.
"Keep your prickly arms down!" the daisies would chant,
But he'd just grin, thinking he's quite the plant!

So in this patch where we bloom and we play,
Nature laughs loud, come join in the fray.
With roots intertwining, and laughter so bright,
Garden giggles echo from morning till night.

Awakening the Soil

A squirrel in pajamas jumped down with a thunk,
Searching for acorns with quite the great funk.
He stumbled on dirt, did a wild little spin,
Crying, "What's this? Where do I begin?"

The earthworms were plotting a soil-themed show,
"Come watch our grand dance, we'll put on a glow!"
But one worm tripped and fell into a hole,
Saying, "I wasn't ready, I'll stick to my role!"

Sunflowers giggled, their heads held up high,
As they waved to a bee that zoomed by the sky.
"I'm busy!" he buzzed, "No stopping for fun!"
Yet he spun in a circle, "Oops! There goes my run!"

So in this patch, where mischief's the game,
Even the roots have laughter to claim.
With smiles all around, and critters in tow,
Awakening the soil, for everyone to grow.

Mosaic of Growth

Once there was a sprout, quite bold and spry,
It wore a big hat, aimed to touch the sky.
"Look at me!" it shouted, "A tree in the making!"
But birds just replied, "It's your breakfast we're taking!"

Nearby, a daffodil tried to play tough,
"I'm no sunny flower! I'm made of pure fluff!"
But a breeze teased her lightly, "Oh darling, please,
With petals like that, you're a floral tease!"

A patch of lilies started a race,
"Let's see who can bloom with the fastest pace!"
But one tipped over, fell flat on its face,
Saying, "That's what I get for a silly embrace!"

In this garden of laughter, where growth meets the jest,
Each bloom finds a friend, and they all feel blessed.
With giggles and colors, a vibrant tableau,
A mosaic of growth, come watch how we glow!

The Embrace of Green

In a jungle parade where the leaves wore ties,
A monkey cracked jokes, oh how time flies!
"This vine is my necktie, just look at my flair!"
And the parrots all joined, "We're green fashion's wear!"

Bamboo held a party, with snacks made of shoots,
The bushes were dancing, in their bright leafy boots.
But a clumsy old cactus spiked everyone's fun,
At first it was laughter, now "Oops! There's a stun!"

Vines tangled up fresh in a laughter-filled mess,
"Help! I've got no boundaries!" a flower confessed.
But together they twirled in their humorous spin,
Creating a tangle, oh, what a win!

So gather your greens, let the giggling commence,
In this embrace of green, life has no pretense.
With nature's own humor, together we thrive,
Blooming in laughter, we feel so alive!

www.ingramcontent.com/pod-product-compliance
Lightning Source LLC
Chambersburg PA
CBHW071820160426
43209CB00003B/138